W9-BTE-621

BUFFALO

RIO NUEVO PUBLISHERS®
P.O. Box 5250, Tucson, Arizona 85703-0250
(520) 623-9558, www.rionuevo.com

Text © 2005 by Win Blevins. See page 64 for photography copyrights. All rights
reserved. No part of this book may be reproduced, stored, introduced into a
retrieval system, or otherwise copied in any form without the prior written
permission of the publisher, except for brief quotations in reviews or citations.

Design: Karen Schober, Seattle, Washington

Library of Congress Cataloging-in-Publication Data

Blevins, Winfred.
Buffalo / Win Blevins.
      p. cm. -- (Look West series)
   ISBN 1-887896-73-2 (hardcover)
   ISBN-13 978-1-887896-73-3 (hardcover)
1. American bison. I. Title. II. Look West
   QL737.U53B575 2005
   599.64'3--dc22

                        2004030626

Printed in Hong Kong
10 9 8 7 6 5 4 3 2 1

BUFFALO

Win Blevins

LOOK WEST
SERIES

RIO NUEVO PUBLISHERS
TUCSON, ARIZONA

FIRST IMAGINE THE SMELL. THE SCENT OF A BUFFALO IS MUSKY,
THICK WITH HINTS THAT ARE MYSTERIOUS TO THE MIND BUT FAMILIAR TO THE
BODY AND THE HEART. A SWIRL OF RICH GRASSES IS HERE, AND THE TANG OF MUD,
SWEAT, AND DUNG, MIXED WITH SOMETHING PRIMEVAL. WHEN YOU DRAW IT INTO
YOUR NOSTRILS, IT GOES NOT TO YOUR REASON BUT TO THE OLD, ATAVISTIC BRAIN,
THE ONE THAT SPEAKS ONLY OF HUNGER, LUST, AND DANGER. YOUR BLOOD
SURGES THROUGH YOUR ARMS AND LEGS AND HEART AND YOU WANT TO…

Old-time cowboys told a story. When some buffalo still ran wild, a lot of the hands wanted to catch a buffalo calf. The bulls and cows were far too unruly, but you could get the little fellows used to you, maybe train them, start a herd. And the easiest way to get calves back to the home ranch, they discovered, was to bend down and

LEFT: *Bison bison,* Yellowstone National Park, Wyoming.
ABOVE: Buffalo nickel (minted 1913–1938).

— 5 —

trade breath with them. Then they would follow you like they followed their mothers.

The same old-timers, however, laughed and said there was never any such thing as a tame buffalo. You could rope it and hold it still. You could pen it up. Sometimes you could ride it, or very occasionally train it to pull a wagon. But that buffalo was still a buffalo. You might keep it in the barn for four nights, or forty, or even four hundred. And on the four hundred and first, if it took a notion, the buffalo would hammer right through your barn wall, knock down the corral, bust through any number of fences, and go wherever it pleased. It would do that any time it felt the urge.

That's the way buffalo were when the last ice age ended, when Plains Indians hunted them and worshipped them, and how they are today. You can never tell. The heart and spirit of a buffalo are *wild*.

SAVVY WESTERNERS STEER CLEAR of the buffalo. The grizzly is awesome but almost always avoids contact with people. The moose is ornery and mean, but lacks the raw power of the buffalo. That power is half of what makes the buffalo so dangerous. The other half is that the animal is absolutely unpredictable.

Buffalo calf in a meadow, Yellowstone National Park, Wyoming.

I have climbed mountains on three continents, fallen into crevasses on glaciers, and survived huge blizzards on high peaks. But the greatest danger I've faced was a surprise up-close introduction to buffalo.

I was riding my bike on a very rough road in Grand Teton National Park, heading down to the Snake River for fun. I came to a sudden downturn, short and steep and deeply rutted and cobbled. At the bottom of the short hill stood the park buffalo herd, looking up at me.

I had a fleeting thought of trying to stop. The bike probably would have skidded onto its side, or hit a hole and sent me over the handlebars. Either way, I would have been lying on my back, dazed, looking up directly into the muzzles of those couple of dozen buffalo, very, very close.

What they would have thought, and done, is unknowable, maybe unthinkable.

I stood up and cranked those pedals as hard as I could. By a miracle I kept my balance. By the beneficence of buffalo, I pedaled right through the herd, zigging and zagging. They were well spaced. Some stopped, but none stepped out of the way. Some gazed curiously at me, and others gazed at whatever interests buffalo more than wheeled maniacs. Maybe buffalo, like Plains Indians, respect madmen and stand back.

When I cleared the herd, I wanted to shout in exultation. That's what you want to do when you dance a waltz with death and come away breathing. But I was afraid to jostle the emotions of the great beasts.

BUFFALO HAVE MADE THIS CONTINENT their home for several hundred thousand years. The scientific name is bison—*Bison latifrons, Bison antiquus, Bison occidentalis, Bison priscus, Bison bison bison,* and *Bison bison athabascae* are the various North American species and subspecies identified, the last two still being with us. Some sticklers want us to call them bison. But we call arachnids "spiders" and homo sapiens "human beings"; by common consent our name for a bison is "buffalo."

Scientists believe that the first buffalo came to North America over the Bering land bridge from Asia somewhere between 200,000 and 800,000 years ago. Those early creatures were bigger than their modern descendants—the horns on some ancient skeletons are six feet across, more than double the span of buffalo these days. These giants lumbered slowly south and east, until they reached Florida, California, and perhaps even Central America.

Plains Indian people of the nineteenth century believed that the buffalo emerged from caves each spring. In the same way that the greening Earth bore new leaves and grasses, the gods provided this infinitely renewable supply of meat.

The Lakota people told a story about it: A long time before the memories of the oldest men, a man who was traveling came upon a hill with many caves. Exploring these passageways, he found buffalo hair on the walls and buffalo tracks on the floor. This, he realized, was where the buffalo lived underground and raised their children. He'd found their secret home.

Prehistoric rock painting of injured bison, Grotte de Niaux, Ariège, Midi-Pyrénées, France.

In another myth, all the buffalo on the planet were owned by a being named Humpback, who kept them for himself. The trickster Coyote changed himself into a dog and was adopted by Humpback's son as a pet. At night Coyote sneaked into the corral and turned all the buffalo loose, and they scattered all over the world.

Hunting Buffalo Camouflaged with Wolf Skins, ca. 1832, colored engraving by George Catlin (1794–1872).

Perhaps there is a kind of truth in both the scientists' and the Indians' stories.

At the same time the buffalo in North America were evolving into *Bison bison* and *Bison bison athabascae,* the Eurasian buffalo (also called the wisent) turned into a taller, longer-legged, and skinnier beast. Like his American cousin, he played a huge role in the life and psyche of another species cohabiting the Earth with him, the human beings of Europe. Lascaux Grotto in France features a series of shamanistic paintings that are among the most admired of all prehistoric art. The central figure is a buffalo with a spear in its belly. In front of the buffalo is a man, the only human being among more than six hundred animals. This impressive bison, according to the student of myth Joseph Campbell, is not a buffalo but "capital B buffalo," the essence or archetype of buffalo.

Human beings on both continents danced and sang and prayed to buffalo.

THE MODERN BUFFALO OF THE GREAT PLAINS is one impressive creature. The bulls stand five or six feet tall at the hump, reach eight to ten feet long, and often weigh a ton or more. The cows stay svelte, weighing only half as much. The animals are usually brown and black, with shaggy fur on their heads and the front halves of their bodies, and small, stringy beards. The calves are red or yellow.

Buffalo have small hindquarters and big forequarters that sup-

port an immense head, which rides low to the ground. Both bulls and cows sport horns. The bulls hang together, away from the cows and calves, except during the mating or "running" season, which begins in mid summer. According to men who have raised them, the animals live from thirty to fifty years, sometimes longer.

Buffalo feed on grasses, especially grama, and process them in compound stomachs. They are dim of sight but

Navajo buffalo moon blanket, wool, from Arizona, American School.

keen of smell. Many a hunter discovered that if you didn't approach a herd from downwind, you could easily set ten thousand animals to stampeding across the prairies.

When they ran free, buffalo had few enemies aside from hunters. Wolves would cut out the weak, the sick, the young, and the elderly. Their main hazards, however, were big rivers, deep snow, and prairie fires. In about 1800 Canadian fur traders saw thousands of carcasses of drowned buffalo in what is now southern Saskatchewan. In one case where the herd broke through ice while crossing, the beaver hunters recorded over seven thousand drowned or mired, and still counting.

ONE OTHER ENEMY REQUIRES MENTION, an enemy of bulls only—other buffalo bulls.

Every spring young bulls would challenge the older males. At stake were leadership of the herd and stature as prime male, which brought with it the pick of the cows. At first these challenges would be tentative, and soon ended. As midsummer approached, and mating, they got serious. A bull who aspired to be king of the hill would throw the gauntlet in the face of the current leader and, along with several other young bulls, attack.

They would charge and head-butt each other ferociously. The bulls would step back dazed, and the earth itself would seem to shake. They would try to gore each other; if one could hook the other in the guts, the fight would end in death. Usually, though, these fights were not fatal. The bulls exhausted each other and retired to fight another day.

John C. Frémont, later known as the Path Finder, witnessed such a fight with his men in the 1840s. Eighteen or twenty bulls were battling desperately. The fight was such chaos that Frémont and his soldiers needed some time to realize that this was a bunch of young bulls ganging up on a single patriarch. The young bulls were fat and sleek, the old one gaunt, weak, and already wounded. After seeing it knocked down several times, the soldiers started shooting at the young bulls at close range. But in their rage the bulls didn't even seem to notice the men. On went the battle, and on and on. Finally the young bulls seems to grasp that they were being fired upon, and they wandered away. The old bull, wrote Frémont, "hobbled off to lie down somewhere."

Wading the Little Missouri River, Theodore Roosevelt National Park, North Dakota.

SURELY FEW ANIMALS EVER THRIVED in their environment better than the buffalo. By the time Europeans arrived and settled, the buffalo filled the continent of North America jam full. They roamed the woodlands of the East and the North, the Great Plains, the high mountains, even the deserts.

By far their favorite landscape was the plains, which had abundant grasses and put up no forests, crags, or defiles to inconvenience the huge herds. There were big rivers, not to mention myriad creeks. The land stretched like an immense dining table—from central Canada to southern Texas, and from the Missouri River to the summits of the Rockies, nothing but grass. What else could a buffalo want?

Naturalists of the time attempted, vainly, to estimate how many buffalo the Great Plains supported at the herds' peak. Forty million was a frequent guess.

What we do know is that buffalo congregated into truly immense herds during the running season. An outfit of wagons headed for Santa Fe to trade in 1839 spent three days cutting through a single herd, traveling fifteen miles a day. The earth itself must have looked like a single huge buffalo robe.

Bison bison calf, Tallgrass Prairie Preserve, Pawhuska, Oklahoma.

In 1869, at about the time the hide hunters started decimating the herds, a company of Kansas militiamen saw a herd on the Solomon River that was at least twenty miles wide and sixty miles long. One of the soldiers said there might have been a hundred thousand buffalo, or a million, or ten million—he had no idea.

These vast herds could be heard miles away. The "roaring" of the buffalo it was called—a sound like thunder, made of the tramping of hundreds of thousands of hoofs and the moaning of the bulls. When they heard that sound, people got the devil out of the way.

When these herds got to creeks, they sometimes drank them dry. For a few minutes the streams did not even trickle.

MEN HUNTED THE BUFFALO from at least the time of the Lascaux paintings in Europe, 13,000–15,000 B.C., and (according to archaeological evidence) from at least 10,000 years ago on the Great Plains of North America.

Probably, from the same times, they worshipped buffalo.

To many Indian peoples, the buffalo were more than a fact of nature. They were a manifestation of the goodness of the gods to mankind, the bounty of an Earth that mothers all creatures. So, at

the same time they hunted the buffalo, they performed ceremonies to maintain good relations with the great creatures, to thank them for their sacrifice of flesh, to bring them close for a hunt, and to implore them to return year after year.

The Lakota (Sioux) people put the buffalo at the center of their worldview. This story is the wellspring of their culture: White Buffalo Woman came to the people many centuries ago in the form of a buffalo who transformed herself into a woman. She bore a great gift—the sacred pipe. She taught the people to respect this pipe and how to use it. She taught them, on that most memorable visit, that the stone bowl of the pipe represents the buffalo, and at the same time represents the flesh and blood of the red man. The buffalo is also the universe and the four directions. He stands on four legs, for the four ages of man. The buffalo holds back the waters. When his legs weaken and fail, this world will end.

INDIANS OF THE GREAT PLAINS hunted the buffalo by many methods. Perhaps the first was the surround, in which the Indians formed a circle around a small group of animals. Then they would run about and yell loudly, all the while closing in and making the cluster of frightened buffalo tighter and tighter. At last, when they judged that the buffalo were sufficiently intimidated by the dense ring of humanity, they let fly their lances and arrows. Often not a single buffalo escaped.

Another method was impounding. The Indians would drive the buffalo down a corridor that got narrower and narrower until it ended in an enclosure, and there kill them.

Hunting Buffalo, 1837, watercolor on paper by Alfred Jacob Miller (1810–74).

Another technique of hunting was to set fires on all sides of a herd but one. When the buffalo fled the flames through the only possible exit, the Indian hunters were waiting.

The buffalo jump was one of the most successful modes of hunting. Here Indian hunters stampeded a herd off a cliff. When the

A Young Arapaho, oil on canvas by Edwin Willard Deming (1860–1942).

front animals tried to stop, the momentum of the beasts behind hurled them off the precipice. Hunters waiting below finished off the wounded. This was a way to get food for a whole tribe for an entire winter.

Over forty years ago Joseph Medicine Crow wrote down an old tale of his Crow people, giving Old Man Coyote, the creator of the world, credit for coming up with the idea of the buffalo jump.

Old Man Coyote got hungry, the story goes, and he saw a buffalo herd near a cliff that was covered with fog. He decided on a trick. He'd challenge the buffalo to a race. Of course the buffalo couldn't resist. At the edge of the cliff Old Man Coyote disappeared, but the buffalo sailed off the edge. Then Old Man Coyote turned up at the bottom looking disheveled and pretending to be hurt. But he got his meal.

WHEN INDIAN PEOPLE got the horse from the Spaniards, their buffalo hunting changed.

First, the horse made them nomadic. Instead of living in fixed locations, they could now roam the plains and camp near the great masses of buffalo. Second, skilled men on horseback could ride alongside a stampeding herd and hurl lances or shoot arrows into their sides, killing many animals.

The buffalo became the main item, almost the only item, in the Plains Indian pantry. They loved to eat the tongues, the humps, the hump ribs, the back straps, the roasts from the big forelegs, the kidneys and liver. They boiled, broiled, roasted, and baked these meats. The fat along the back, dried, was a delicacy; so was kidney fat.

They dried much of this meat to preserve it until the next hunt. The method was to build wooden racks high enough to keep the dogs off, cut the flesh into long strips, and expose it to the wind and sun for several days. A low, smoky fire speeded up the drying and added a good flavor. The result was what white folks call jerky.

Their favorite way to preserve buffalo meat, by far, was to make it into pemmican. You pulverized the jerky by pounding it, then stuffed it into a buffalo-skin bag. Next, you poured melted fat over it. If you had any dried berries, you mixed them in. Then you sewed the bag shut for future use. In this form pemmican would last for years.

Though Plains Indian people also gathered roots, berries, and other wild plants, and took other animals such as elk and deer, their

Buffalo dance, San Ildefonso Pueblo, New Mexico.

diet is estimated to have been 90 percent or more buffalo meat. And they were splendidly healthy.

The buffalo gave them much more than meat. They used the hides, with the hair on, for bedding and for coats and hats. With the hair scraped off, the hides made covers for tipis and sweat lodges; they also furnished material for bags, boxes called parfleches, and other items. Sinew provided thread. The hooves were turned into glue or rattles. The horns became cups. The thick hide of the face made a good shield. A whole hide made a fine surface for painting, and a tribal historian kept records of the years with paintings that represented important events. Altogether the buffalo was a red man's general store on the ramble.

The Plains Indians repaid the buffalo with gratitude and devotion. That devotion abounds in their art. We can still see the painted buffalo skulls and the bowls of sacred pipes carved in the shape of buffalo. I also love what is called ledger art. These drawings were done with colored pencils in traders' ledger books when the great herds were disappearing or gone. Even then, the painters continued to render the subjects that inspired their deepest feelings, men engaged in the practical craft and sacred art of hunting buffalo.

THE FIRST WHITE MEN TO TRAVEL the Great Plains, the mountain men, learned to hunt them from the Indians, on horseback. In fact they often hunted with Indians and found the buffalo hunt the experience of a lifetime.

You approach from downwind, to have a chance to get close. At some point a bull sniffs you, or sees your movement, and sounds a warning. Suddenly, the herd is off in the other direction, running into the wind, a gargantuan mass of four-footed bestiality gone mad.

Off you go behind them, as fast as possible, and you ride in among the great beasts themselves. The roar is incredible. Perhaps modern readers have stood between cars on a fast-moving train, or floated a big rapid in a small boat—these cacophonies only hint at the din that now fills the hunter's ears.

The ground is uneven, cut by ravines, pitted by prairie dog holes. If your horse loses its footing, it will probably break a leg, and you will get trampled. For this herd at stampede is a mindless creature, intent on nothing but running and running and running, caring not a fig for whatever stands in the way.

Dust rages all around. You cannot see anything but a hurricane of dirt churned up by thousands of hoofs. It chokes your throat and

Theodore Roosevelt National Park, North Dakota.

blinds your eyes. Through the dust appear great hulking shapes of buffalo on the run, hindquarters and forequarters rising up and down rhythmically. However big you thought they were, you now realize they are more massive, faster, and wilder. You have cast your life like a leaf into a storm.

But your heart is wild for buffalo. With your knees you guide your horse toward a certain cow you can barely make out. The experienced horse brings you up alongside. This is your chance. You raise your rifle, sight at a spot in the brisket just behind the shoulder, and fire.

Regardless of result, you hurtle onward, borne madly by the will of the herd and by your own exultation. You realize that you are shouting for all your lungs are worth and cannot even hear your own voice.

Drunk with the ecstasy of the chase, you steer your horse toward another animal and shoot again, and again, and again, until the horse can run no more, or your powder horn is empty.

You ride back through the down beasts and help with the skinning. If you are an old hand, you eat the liver raw.

That night you feast on hump ribs, or tongue, or whatever you fancy. If you are like most whites, whether mountain man or emigrant, the flesh of buffalo seems the finest meat you ever tasted.

Wichita Mountains National Wildlife Refuge, Oklahoma.

If you are hunting with Indians, you may get a special treat. A woman will turn a section of gut inside out, stuff it with chopped meat and spices, and broil it on a stick. Almost everyone who ever tasted the result, called *boudins,* found the taste beyond compare.

This hunting was more than an exhilarating sport. It was a healthy relationship between man and beast—as long as man sought the flesh only for food.

IN LESS THAN A CENTURY, amazingly, a different kind of hunting reduced these great herds to ragtag remnants. In the early 1800s Indian people began to kill buffalo not for food but for trade. They had discovered that the fur traders would pay well for the hides and tongues, and for jerky and pemmican. In 1850 about 100,000 buffalo hides came down the river to St. Louis. Killing for profit had arrived.

Immediately after the Civil War, the railroads hired hunters like Buffalo Bill Cody to shoot buffalo to feed the rail-laying crews. Hard-working laborers required lots of meat.

The real destruction of the herds, however, started when experiments showed that buffalo hides made good leather. Cowhides were no longer pouring in via ships from California, and Eastern

manufacturers demanded raw material for everything they could make from hides, from shoes to suitcases. Thus arrived the men who slaughtered for riches.

These buffalo runners, as they called themselves, did not love the hunt. They didn't ride among the herds but used ultra-powerful rifles at long distances, trying to down as many buffalo as possible without spooking a herd.

In 1872 a Kansas newspaper estimated that two thousand of these men were hunting in western Kansas alone, killing an average of fifteen buffalo a day. They sold the meat in nearby towns for one and a half or two cents—that's *cents*—per pound, and the hides for an average of two dollars each. The life of a buffalo, which was everything to the Indian, in the white man's ledger was worth three dollars.

One buffalo runner calculated it in the coldest of terms: The plains were home to twenty million buffalo worth three dollars or more each—a total of sixty million dollars. Since cartridges cost a quarter at the most, each buffalo returned his investment twelve times over. Even after including other costs, a hunter could net $6,000 a month, three times what the President of the United

Sunrise in Hayden Valley, Yellowstone National Park, Wyoming.

States earned. "Was I not lucky," he wrote, "that I discovered this quick and easy way to fortune?"

Custer State Park in South Dakota supports about 2,000 buffalo.

In the 1880s the buffalo runners, having decimated the herds of the Southern Plains, repeated the process on the Northern Plains.

A figure who seems an eloquent symbol now arrived. The bone picker wandered the plains where the great herds had once thrived, collecting the bones, horns, and hoofs. Back in the East these would be ground up to make fertilizer or glue, or to be used in the refining of sugar.

Certainly there were protests while this slaughter went on. Men made attempts to get Congress to pass laws to save the buffalo. Some states tried to pass laws, and Wyoming did pass one (but could not enforce it). One powerful interest dictated the demise of the buffalo: Westerners in the West knew, and the army knew, and the federal government knew, that the buffalo was the entire livelihood of the Indian.

Eliminate the buffalo, they said in their privy councils, and you will make the Indian into a farmer. You will civilize him. You will make him a white man.

Some of them said, in greater privacy, eliminate the buffalo and you eliminate the Indian.

Thus the fate of the great herds.

THE BUFFALO, HOWEVER, declined the invitation to become extinct.

A number of people saw what was happening and took action. A Flathead Indian named Samuel Walking Coyote started raising thirteen buffalo in the Flathead Valley. Neighboring white ranchers bought Walking Coyote's buffalo, plus some other buffalo, and established a larger herd.

In Kansas a rancher named Buffalo Jones started his own herd. Charles Goodnight, a prominent rancher in the Texas Panhandle, set about raising buffalo and cattalo, a cross made by breeding a buffalo bull to a beef cow. (Goodnight believed that buffalo were a panacea, capable of curing arthritis and many other ailments.) In 1881 Pete Dupree, a Lakota descended in part from a French fur trapper, started a herd on the Cheyenne River.

In 1905 the American Bison Society was founded in New York City, of all places, and began to work to get the federal government to create buffalo ranges. Over the next decade herds were established in Yellowstone National Park, Montana, Oklahoma, Nebraska, South Dakota, and even North Carolina.

In the end, though, the men and women who saved the buffalo were ranchers.

Feeding near geysers in Yellowstone National Park.

IT IS AN IRONY that these ranchers, who once wanted the buffalo out of the way for their cattle, saved the buffalo by raising them as they raised cows.

Buffalo in captivity were nothing new. Franciscan monks raised them in Mexico in the 1600s. The mountain man Uncle Dick Wootton had a herd in the 1840s. A nineteenth-century rancher in Lexington, Kentucky, kept a herd for three decades. All these ranchers seem to have learned the same lessons. Buffalo are fundamentally intractable—they do what they want to do when they want to do it. No fence can hold them. They bull their way through almost anything and are great jumpers, known even to leap over pickup trucks. And in the end, no man owns a buffalo.

The early ranchers kept buffalo to try to train them as draft animals, or to display them, or for nostalgia. Those approaches, however, were expensive. The buffalo at last was saved because it whipped its main nemesis, the dollar. At some point ranchers discovered a market for buffalo meat. Now the commercial value of buffalo, which nearly killed them all, has saved the species and is increasing buffalokind.

As of this year, 2004, buffalo ranches in the United States are raising about 232,000 head; add in the buffalo in public herds and you get over a quarter million animals. Canadian ranchers are raising another 150,000 to 200,000.

Buffalo in spring molt, Lamar Valley, Yellowstone National Park.

These ranchers have saved the species. Most of them, like their predecessors in the nineteenth century, do it more as a labor of love than to turn a profit (though they like doing that too, when they can).

Red Canyon Ranch, near Thermopolis, Wyoming, is a good example. Michael and Kathleen Gear, my longtime friends and authors of the best-selling First North Americans series *(People of the Wolf, People of the Raven),* are entranced by buffalo. Sure, it's a business for them. They raise animals for meat, and they raise them as breeding stock. Since they started entering their animals in shows five years ago, they've won fifty-three trophies, and in 2004 Red Canyon Ranch was named Producer of the Year at a Denver exhibition.

Now when I see Kathleen and Michael, their stories are rampant with buffalo. The buffalo calf who jumped up on their bed. The calf Slipper, an orphan who was hugely curious about the world and left it at the age of five days. The bull that refuses to be separated from his favorite cows—and his bullish ways of stating his will. They are full of pride and a kind of dazzled happiness.

"Buffalo today are more exciting than buffalo then," says Michael.

Annual buffalo roundup, Custer State Park, South Dakota.

The world has reason to be grateful to ranchers like the Gears, who continue to keep a marvelous species alive. I'm tickled to see a splendid bull penned within fences or munching on a flake of hay, or a fine cow with an ear tag. Then I remember the herds that were twenty miles long and sixty miles wide, and am saddened.

Buffalo roundup, National Bison Range, Montana.

RECENTLY THE PLAINS INDIANS have discovered a new source of hope on a Wisconsin farm.

For centuries the white buffalo have been revered by the Native peoples of the Great Plains, especially by the Lakota (Sioux), whose great mythic story centers on White Buffalo Woman.

When Indians from the buffalo-hunting tribes saw white buffalo, they slew the animals and dressed their hides with reverence. Pawnees wrapped their medicine bundles in robes from white buffalo. Cheyenne warriors carried white buffalo robes into battle, believing the robes would protect them. Blackfoot medicine men used white buffalo robes in healing ceremonies. Blackfeet also hung robes of white buffalo near the tipis of medicine men as an offering to Sun.

A buffalo did not have to be pure white to be a power object. Cream-colored buffalo, dappled buffalo, even animals with white heads only were regarded as powerful medicine.

Once no Indian from a buffalo-hunting tribe would part with a white buffalo robe at any price. As the nineteenth century progressed, some came into the hands of white folks, as gifts or purchases. Perhaps the old gods were failing, including the white buffalo.

Anglos also attributed power to the white buffalo. Two hunters, James Caspion and Sam Tillman, were riding through western Kansas looking for buffalo in 1871. They rode well apart, so that each could see a wide range of country. Caspion spotted a large herd, and in it was a milk-white buffalo.

Just then Cheyennes attacked Tillman and took his scalp. Then they started toward Caspion. Desperate, he rode into the herd and stampeded it.

Caspion could see nothing in the turmoil of dust. His horse was uncontrollable. He gave the mount its head, held on, and hoped. For hours and hours they ran headlong. At nightfall he could tell by the feel of the ground that they were in hilly country, at least twenty-five miles from where they started. The herd divided, part of them sweeping Caspion into a valley. The dust was less, and Caspion could see the animals around him under a full, bright moon. He was running near the white buffalo.

When the herd slowed, Caspion stopped and slept. The next morning he rode back along the trail of the stampede. At one point some buffalo had fallen into a ravine and been killed or injured. There, with a broken leg, stood the white buffalo, a bull.

Waiting out a spring rain, Madison River area, Yellowstone National Park.

Caspion shot it, skinned it, and kept the hide as his good luck talisman.

Five years later, on a drunken binge, he sold the hide. Shortly thereafter he was killed by Comanches.

In August of 1994, at the Janesville, Wisconsin, farm of the Dave Heider family, a pure white buffalo calf was born. Miracle, as the family named her, was a heifer.

Quickly, Plains Indian people declared that she was a sign. No white calf, they believed, had been born since 1933. Indian people and many others proclaimed her a sign of renewal, hope, and harmony between all peoples. Some Lakotas believe her to be a sign of the imminent return of White Buffalo Woman.

The family, acknowledging the calf as a gift to all peoples, permitted viewing of Miracle every day. Thousands of people went to see her or to pray. Artists made their tributes to her.

The four directions, which are invoked perpetually in Lakota prayers, are associated with distinct colors—red for the east, yellow for the south, black for the west, and white for the north. In many Lakota stories a sacred creature appears to people and changes through the four colors, demonstrating that it is a sacred being. In

Confrontation with a bull elk in rut, dense fog, Elk Park, Yellowstone National Park.

the first three years of her life, Miracle changed from her birth color, white, to black, then yellow, then red.

Miracle died in 2004. Pictures of her in each color are posted on her website at www.home stead.com/WhiteBuffaloMiracle/.

Arvol Looking Horse, the keeper of the White Buffalo Woman pipe for the Lakota tribe, issued this statement, among others, about Miracle:

"We are now in a time of prophecy: Animal Nations would stand upon Mother Earth a different color than their natural being and be born white. They are speaking to us with the only voice that can be heard. These messages are of a blessing and yet a great warning!

Buffalo bladder pouch, traditionally used to hold porcupine needles.

"It is a time of great urgency to unite for Peace and Harmony upon Mother Earth in order for our future generations to survive.

"Mother Earth is not a resource, but rather the source of life itself."

PERHAPS EACH OF US WHO LOVES the buffalo has his own personal story about the marvelous creature—and his own dream about it. Mine goes like this:

Maybe, somewhere, a herd of wild buffalo still ranges the prairies, the woodlands, or the mountains. In the Northwest Territories, perhaps. There the land itself is still wild, few human beings go, and the earth-moving machines have not yet intruded. Or perhaps in Alaska.

These buffalo, in my dream, have never seen cattle. Nor did their ancestors see them. They have no contact with human beings, except perhaps for a few local hunters, either red men or white, who know of the herd, love it, and partly out of love take an occasional animal for meat or for their own ceremonies—Sun Dance, Christmas, or any other occasion.

The herd does nothing except what buffalo have always done. The bulls and cows mate in season. They take their fill of the green

Buffalo cow and calf crossing the Madison River, Yellowstone National Park.

grasses of summer and the brown ones of autumn. In the winter they use their great heads like shovels, just as their ancestors did, and find their way to grass enough to survive. In the spring they welcome the greening up with eager bellies.

They rub themselves against trees. They roll in wallows and come away muddy, a way of getting cool and keeping insects off. They run, just for the fun of it.

When the time comes, the young bulls challenge the old ones. The ground trembles with the fury of their battles. Eventually, this year or the next or the one after that, the young bulls win and claim their rights among the cows. The old hover on the edges of the herd, disgraced, or wander off and are never seen again.

The herd goes on.

No, these buffalo are not particularly useful, in the ways we generally think of use. They contribute nothing to the economy. They are not studied by scientists to become bits of information in treatises. They do not pull wagons or in any other way behave in ways that we direct.

They simply are. They exist as part of the cornucopia of life created and nurtured by our mother the Earth. In that abundance

every living thing supports every other, yet each exists for its own sake. Because all forms of life are good, and all forms are beautiful.

Such is my dream.

Buffalo herd stampede, Red Sleep Mountain, National Bison Range, Montana.

Hayden Valley, Yellowstone National Park.

BUFFALO AT A GLANCE

NORTH AMERICAN SPECIES, PAST AND PRESENT Extinct species include *Bison latifrons* (to 120,000 years ago), *Bison antiquus* (about 120,000 to 10,000 years ago), and *Bison occidentalis* (120,000 years ago to its development into the two modern species—the plains buffalo and the woodland buffalo). The plains buffalo (*Bison bison*) lived primarily on the Great Plains, and the woodland buffalo (*Bison bison athabascae*) lived primarily in the Rocky Mountains. (The European bison, called the wisent, is taller than the American buffalo but not as solid and thick. Only a few herds of this species survive.)

NAMES *Bison bison* have been called "buffalo" since the early 18th century. Early Spanish explorers called them *cibola, bisonte,* or *armenta.* French colonists and fur traders called them *Bison d'Amerique* or *boeuf,* and the Lakota Sioux called them *tatanka*.

PHYSICAL CHARACTERISTICS The buffalo has a big, heavy head that is carried low. Both male and female have horns. The buffalo has a definite hump at the shoulder, and a bull is generally 5 to 6 (or more) feet tall at that point. Bulls weigh about one ton, cows about 700 pounds. Buffalo have dark brown fur that is thick in winter but is generally shed in the hot months. Buffalo smell and hear well, but see dimly.

LIFE CYCLES A buffalo cow gives birth to only one calf per year and cares for it during the first year of its life. Mating season is late June through September, with babies born the following spring. Life expectancy is 20 to 40 years, sometimes even 50.

DIET Bison graze primarily on grasses, mostly in the mornings and evenings, and take water only once a day.

BEHAVIOR Buffalo communicate vocally with grunts and snorts. Buffalo bulls stage head-butting battles for dominance of the herd and can run up to 30 miles per hour.

POPULATION Hunting of the buffalo for hides nearly brought the animals to extinction in the 1870s and 1880s. Now more than 400,000 are being raised in North America.

WHERE YOU CAN SEE BUFFALO

Antelope Island State Park, Utah
Badlands National Park, South Dakota
Bison Prairie 1, Ho-Chunk Nation, Wisconsin
Blue Mounds State Park, Minnesota
Bronx Zoo, New York
Buffalo Rock State Park, Illinois
Caprock Canyons State Park and Trailway, Quitaque, Texas

Catalina Island, California

Cross Ranch Nature Preserve, North Dakota

Custer State Park, South Dakota

Daniels Park and Genesee Park, Denver, Colorado

Golden Gate Park, San Francisco, California

Grand Teton National Park, Wyoming

Henry Mountains Wilderness, Utah

Hot Springs State Park, Wyoming

Land between the Lakes National Recreation Area, Kentucky

Nambe Pueblo, New Mexico

Oakland Zoo, Oakland, California

Picuris Pueblo, New Mexico

National Bison Range, Moiese, Montana

The National Buffalo Museum, Jamestown, North Dakota

Neal Smith National Wildlife Refuge/Prairie Learning Center,
    Jasper County, Iowa

Raymond Ranch Wildlife Area, Arizona

Sandia Pueblo, New Mexico

Tallgrass Prairie Preserve, Pawhuska, Oklahoma

Taos Pueblo, New Mexico

Tesuque Pueblo, New Mexico

Theodore Roosevelt National Park, North Dakota

Wichita Mountains National Wildlife Refuge, Oklahoma

Wildlife Prairie State Park, Peoria, Illinois

Wind Cave National Park, South Dakota

Yellowstone National Park, Wyoming

SUGGESTED READING

The most valuable book about buffalo for the general reader, by far, is David A. Dary's *The Buffalo Book: The Full Saga of the American Animal* (Swallow Press/Ohio University Press, 1989).

Also useful is Valerius Geist's *Buffalo Nation: History and Legend of the North American Bison* (Voyageur Press, 1996).

A good source for information on contemporary buffalo is the National Bison Association. See bisoncentral.com on the Internet.

PHOTOGRAPHY © AS FOLLOWS:

Erwin and Peggy Bauer/Wildstock: pages 32, 35, 46, 56, 57

Christine L. Humphreys: pages 8, 42, 48, 61

Layne Kennedy: pages 5, 17, 21, 38, 45, 52

Barbara Magnuson and Larry Kimball: pages 18, 51, 54

Mary Ann McDonald: page 4

Jeffrey Rich Nature Photography: pages 7, 41

Joel Sartore: pages 2-3, 28

Stephen Trimble: back cover, pages 27, 31

Dave Welling: front cover, page 1

Bob Young: pages 37, 58

Images on pages 11, 12, 14, 23, and 24 courtesy of Bridgeman Art Library and used with permission; image on page 12 from collection of Bibliotheque Nationale, Paris, France, Lauros/Giraudon; image on page 14 from a private collection, Bolton Picture Library; image on page 23 © Walters Art Museum, Baltimore, Maryland; image on page 24 © Butler Institute of American Art, Youngstown, Ohio, museum purchase 1920.